Copyright © 2014 by Dennis Serra

All rights reserved. This book or any portion thereof may not be reproduced or used in any manner whatsoever without the express written permission of the publisher except for the use of brief quotations in a book review.

Printed in the United States of America

First Printing, 2014

ISBN-13: 978-1496129611

ISBN-10: 149612961X

Dennis Serra

coach@dennisserra.com

www.DennisSerra.com

Dedication

To Michael and Alec.

The Diamond Formation Power Run System for Youth Football
Second Edition

By

Dennis Serra

Table of Contents

Introduction……………………….. 1

Base Formation……………...… 4

Base Assignments…………..… 6

Fullbacks (2 and 4)…………..… 6

Halfback (back 3)……................ 6

Quarterback…………………….. 8

Ends (X and Y)………………….. 9

Linemen………………………….. 9

Using what we know so far…..13

Advanced calls…………………17

Cross Block………………....…17

Offset Formation……………….18

Beast Formation…….................21

Split Formation…….…………... 24

Spread Formation………………26

Combining Formations……….. 27

Triple Threat……………………..28

Your Turn ……………………….. 33

The Diamond Formation Power Run System is more than a mere playbook highlighting a single formation. It is a system of teaching a youth football team a dynamic and effective offense in the most efficient manner. As a youth football coach I found that we have a limited amount of time to teach a youth football team everything they need to know about the game prior to the start of the season. As a coach you will find your team will be a mix of returning players who can quickly get up to speed and first year players who need a great deal of guidance. With this system you can teach the entire team the offense quickly, install confidence, and have your team play faster come game day.

In the Diamond Formation Power Run System you will first be introduced to the base formation and the initial assignments for each position. Second we will add formation variations to take advantage of different situations that may arise during a game. Finally we will review the playbook and play calling strategies.

By starting with one formation at first you will find the team adapts to it quickly and even first year players will get comfortable with their assignments with fewer practices. It's a mistake to try to teach a youth football team numerous formations too fast and expect them to run them with great confidence and enthusiasm.

Your aim should be to create confident and enthusiastic players and eliminate confusion. A confident player will run their assignments without hesitation. An enthusiastic player will put forth a greater effort. A confused player does neither. Confident and enthusiastic teams play faster! When a youth football player has to learn multiple formations they spend more time trying to memorize where they should stand before the play starts and less time thinking about their assignment when the ball is snapped. Practice time is limited in youth football and optimizing your time is essential. You have to ask yourself if you want players spending practice time on where to stand or do you want to use that time improving the speed at which your team plays?

Don't be fooled into thinking that having one base formation makes it easy for defenses to predict your next move! This system will teach the team, and its coach, multiple plays that keep the defense off balance and makes your offense unpredictable. But more on play calling later in the book.

With this system you will teach your players their base assignments from the base formation first. Later you will introduce additional formations to create more dynamic looks, but only when the players are comfortable with their current assignments. The base assignments are often phrased simply like "Do X until Y happens then do Z instead." Breaking down their assignment like this makes learning easier, quicker, and installs confidence in their ability to execute their assignment. For example, a fullback is instructed to: "If a play is called to your side, and you are not running the ball, lead block into the called gap. If the play is called to the opposite side then crash the line and prevent backside pursuit."

The Diamond Formation is a three back formation designed to attack anywhere on the field with a power running game. This formation has been called 'The Inverted Wishbone' or 'Full House' depending on which team is running it. With two full backs and two tight ends in its base formation it can attack both sides of the defense and outnumber them at the point of attack. However, it is also easy to run misdirection plays away from the power run game to keep a defense off balance. The misdirection plays are a key to its success as a defense who keys the power running will find itself out of position when a misdirection play is run.

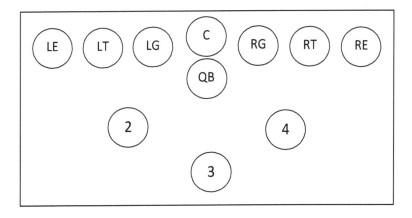

Base Formation:

The Diamond Formation is a double tight three back formation. It has the 2 back 3-4 yards from the line of scrimmage between the left tackle and left guard. The 4 back is also 3-4 yards from the line of scrimmage between the right tackle and right guard and should be even with the 2 back. The 3 back is directly behind the quarterback about 4-5 yards from the line of scrimmage and always about 1 yard back from the 2 and 4 back.

Base play calling is simple. Call the number of the runner first then the number of the gap to be run through. For example a '36' looks like this:

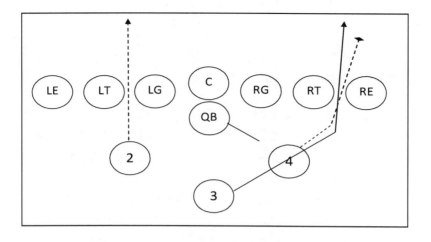

You can expand the play name if you like. 36 Pitch, 36 Gold, or anything that strikes you. There are plays not to the backs. For example the Left End is also known as 'X' and the Right End is known as 'Y.' This will become important later in the system when plays are called for them.

Base assignments:

Running Backs 2 and 4 (Fullbacks): The 2 and 4 backs are responsible for their side of the field. Back 2 for the odd numbered gaps (1, 3, 5, and 7) and back 4 for the even numbered gaps (2, 4, 6, and 8). If a play is called to their side, and they are not running the ball, they must lead block into the called gap. If the play is to the opposite side they must crash towards the line to prevent any penetration by the defense and stop backside pursuit.

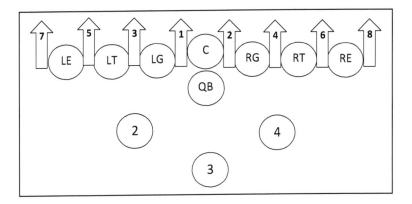

Running Back 3: As a general rule the running back 3 will run a fake away from a 2 or 4 back who is running the ball unless a 'Lead' is called. With a 3 back, who is generally your best back, having him run away from the play can cause the opposing linebackers to slide towards his direction causing a hole in the second layer of the defense for the runner.

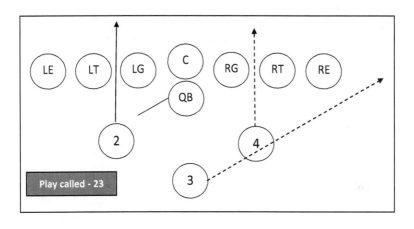

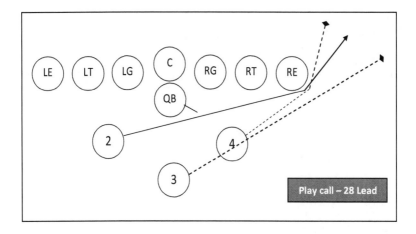

Quarterback (QB): The QB will turn towards the play when handing off or pitching the ball (2, 4, 6, 8 hole to the right and 1, 3, 5, 7 hole to the left) unless a fake is called then the QB turns towards the fake.

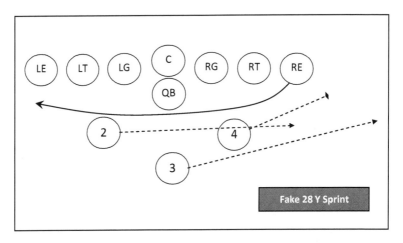

Fake 28 Y Sprint

In the above play, Fake 28 Y Sprint, the QB first pivots to the right as all three backs go right as well. Imagine you are the opposing middle linebacker. All three backs are traveling to your left and the QB pivots to his left, as he usually does to pitch it to the three back or hand it off to the 2 back for a power sweep. You know from past plays the offense is trying to overload the defense to your left so you begin to sprint to cut the runner off. Suddenly, the right end (Y) pivots and runs underneath the running backs and takes the ball from the QB.

Ends (LE or X and RE or Y): The Ends will function like blockers unless a play is called to them. A typical play is the 'Fake 28 Y Sprint.'

Linemen (LT, LG, C, RG, and RT): Offensive Linemen have a rule set they follow for their blocking assignments. To have a blocking scheme for each play will prove too daunting for a youth football player. If you can break their assignment down to a set of rules to follow it becomes much easier. Again, we want the players to play fast and not be bogged down by complicated blocking assignments. The faster a youth football player comprehends his assignment the more confident and *aggressively* they will execute that assignment. I cannot stress this enough.

The rules are:

1. **Play side Gap** – If the play is called to your right and a defender is lined up in the gap to your right – block that defender.
2. **Man Up** – If rule one does not apply block the player lined up over you.
3. **Inside Gap** – If rules one and two do not apply, block the player in your inside gap. The gap closest to the Center. Remember, your play side gap and the inside gap maybe the same gap.

4. **Wrecking Ball** – If no one is in your play side gap, lined up over you, or in your inside gap, you are the wrecking ball. Wrecking Balls can bounce off of defensive linemen and then go to the second level and find a Linebacker to block.

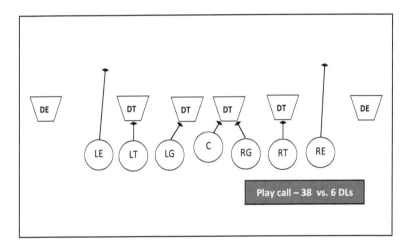

Play call – 38 vs. 6 DLs

When the linemen are facing 6 defensive linemen (common in youth tackle football) the rules will have blocks as seen above. The blocking progression for each player is as follows:

Left End (**LE**) – 1) No one to the play side gap. 2) No one over the LE. 3) No one in the inside gap (same gap as the play side gap). 4) Wrecking Ball. On the way to the 2nd level of the defense he can scrap block the DT over the LT.

Left Tackle (**LT**) – 1) No one to the play side gap. 2) A DT man up over the LT.

Left Guard (**LG**) – 1) A DT to the play side gap (right).

Center (**C**) – 1) A DT to the play side gap.

Right Guard (**RG**) – 1) No one in the play side gap. 2) No one over the RG. 3) A DT in the inside gap.

Right Tackle (**RT**) – 1) No one to the play side gap. 2) A DT lined up over the RT.

Right End (**RE**) – 1) No one to the play side gap (the DE is too far away). 2) No one over the RE. 3) No one in the inside gap. 4) Wrecking Ball. On the way to the 2nd level of the defense he can scrap block the DT over the RT.

Notice the ends do not have the first three blocking rules apply to them so they become our wrecking balls. They seek out a linebacker to block. The Left End (LE) ignores the Defensive End (DE) to his left as the defender is not in the play side gap, over him, or in the inside gap. Remember back 2's assignment? Back 2 will cut off backside pursuit as the play is not to his side. So if the DE sprints to the backfield to follow our runner he will be met by back 2.

I know the RE not blocking the DE on the right side bothers you. At first glance it should as we do not want anyone unblocked. However, the rules are set up as to never have our linemen perform a 'reach block.' The DE is not lined up over the RE's outside shoulder so he is not in the play side gap. He is too far away. So the RE seeks out a linebacker. Remember back 4's assignment? He is lead blocking and will have a full head of steam to kick out the DE creating a natural hole for the runner.

The blocking rules against five defensive linemen are similar. I don't mind having my line double teaming defensive linemen. In youth football the weights between players are so similar that a double team should result in your linemen pushing the defender into the second level and disrupting pursuing linebackers. Teach linemen to drive their defender back and make it clear to them that a double team should result in a greater push.

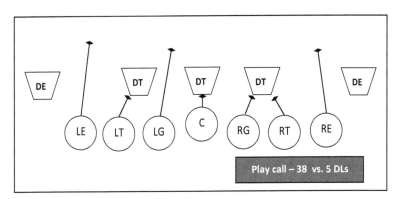

Play call – 38 vs. 5 DLs

Using what we know so far:

Now the players know the base formation and their base assignments. On the surface it seems to be a simple playbook so far, but we already have many choices to throw at a defense. Imagine this sequence of plays designed to test the edges of the defense:

1. 36
2. 47 Lead
3. Fake 28 Y Sprint

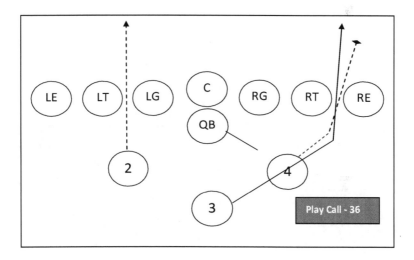

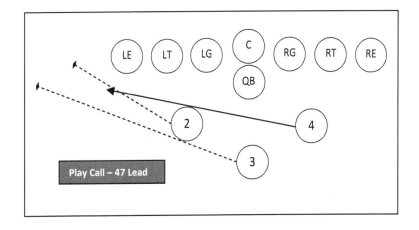

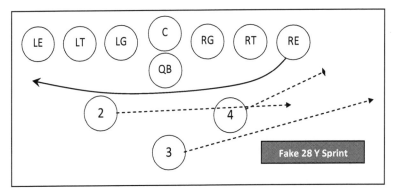

This is a simple series of plays that your team can learn quickly. On 1st down we have the 3 back following a lead block through the 6 hole. Next, the power sweep, the 4 back follows the lead blocks of the 2 and 3 backs to the outside. This play is an attempt to overpower the defense at the point of attack. The third play in the sequence takes advantage of over pursuing line backers as all three backs sprint right, the QB pivots right, and the RE pivots left, takes the handoff, and runs against the grain to the left. All of this is run from the base formation with simple assignments.

Each team learns at a different pace, but what you have seen so far is very basic and, most importantly, easy to learn. However, because this simple system is easy to learn it will have your players executing the plays with great confidence as they will be comfortable with the offense. Also, we can see from the three play sequence that just because this system is easy to learn does not mean it is easy to defend. This is where your play calling comes into play. As a coach you need to be familiar with the plays that are capable from this system. The Diamond Formation Power Run System is not only simple for your players to learn, but also simple for a coach to learn.

When I call plays I like to establish a norm. First I play to my team's strength and observe how the defense reacts. If the defense struggles to get the proper support at the point of attack then very little needs to be changed as they will struggle to stop our offense. If they are aggressive in their pursuit to the ball then it is time to throw a misdirection play at them. This may or may not result in a big gain. However, when done enough the defense will cease to aggressively pursue and hesitate as they try to read the play. This is where your "simple" offense will get the defense back on their heels.

One of the main points of installing this offense was to get our team to play with a high amount of confidence. Confident players play faster! Your players will run their well-rehearsed-simple-assignments with great confidence and attack the play at *full speed*.

If the defense hesitates and tries to read the play they will get beat at the point of attack. If the defensive players are superior athletes to your offensive players they will be able to prevent big gains, but they will not be able to prevent the steady and tiring grind of an attacking offense as they eat up yards and time on the clock. Don't be afraid of having long drives. Many new youth football coaches get frustrated when they do not have big gains. Do not get frustrated.

We had played a team that only ran their best running back and only ran wide sweeps with him (now that was a simple offense). Granted this kid was a great athlete and very fast, but we won the game as we were prepared to grind out their defense and keep them on their heels while our defense made a simple adjustment by widening their contain players.

Do not be predictable and you should be willing to grind out a defense if need be.

Once your team masters the base formation and their assignments it is time to move on to more advanced features of this system.

Advanced formation and blocking calls:

Your team is now playing their base assignments fast and with great confidence. Now it is time to expand the formation and take advantage of defenses that are slow to adjust to change.

Cross Block. Once the linemen understand the basic rules of blocking assignments introduce advanced blocking calls. One such call is the Cross Block. Add this rule: *When a running play is called to the 5 or 6 gap (off-tackle) the End and Tackle perform a Cross Block.*

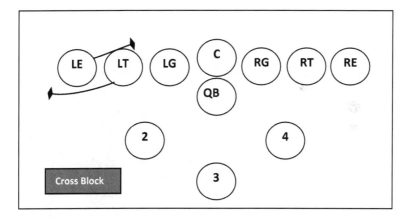

A cross block is when a pair of offensive linemen exchange assignments. Simply put the outside lineman blocks down on the interior lineman's defensive counterpart and the interior lineman pivots and performs a pulling block. Any two linemen can perform this maneuver and it can be quite effective.

On an off-tackle run through the 5 gap the Left End blocks down on the defensive tackle and the Left Offensive Tackle pivots to his left and pulls down the line. Usually the OT will be on a collision course with the defensive end.

When run properly the 5 gap becomes a larger hole for the runner to get through and removes the first layer of the defense.

Offeset formation (*I would rename this formation to whatever your team name is: Bear, Raider, Mustang. Just to make it easier to remember for your team.*). This can be called to the left or right. This is a great formation call and only the tackles have to adjust. When you have only the tackles adjusting then everyone else has no extra assignments to remember. This makes the Offset formation easy to introduce into your play calling. On an Offset Left call (or Raider Left if you will) the RT lines up between the LT and LG. On an Offset Right call the LT would line up between the RG and RT.

Always keep your Ends on the end. Do not leave the end of the line 'uncovered' otherwise you can be called for a penalty. A line is considered 'uncovered' when a non-eligible lineman is on the end of the line. However, check with your organization's rule book to make sure. Many youth football organizations use the high school football rules for their state, plus a few changes, which can differ from standard college or professional rules.

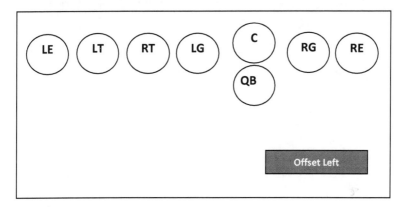

Use the Offset formation to further outnumber the defense. Imagine a call of "Raider Left 37 Pitch." This call will create an extra offensive lineman for the defense to deal with. I have seen youth football defenses slow to adjust to an offset line or defenses that have not been instructed how to react at all.

Do not be afraid to call a play to the weak side of an offset line if the defense starts to overcompensate. If the defense shifts and no longer outnumbers you to the weak side try calling a "Offset left Fake 37, 16 keeper." This will have your 3 back sprinting left into the offset line while the QB is following the lead block of back 4.

When defenses would overcompensate on a short yardage situation a favorite play of mine was "Offset Left 44 Dive." The defense would usually shift their linemen towards the offset side leaving a quick strait forward dive type play effective. Remember the 3 backs base assignment when a "Lead" is not called? He will be running a natural fake away from the play called and the middle linebacker would often follow back 3. This can lead to running space for the 4 back on the second level of the defense.

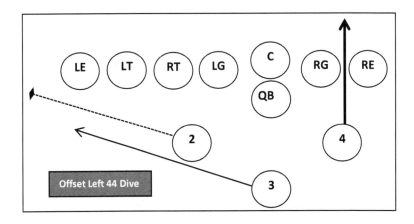

Offset lines in youth football can be very effective. If a defense does not practice what to do against an offset line they will be outnumbered at the point of attack.

As a mental exercise and a learning tool for you as coach get a pencil and paper and draw up (or imagine) the following calls out of the Offset formation:

Offset Right 28 Lead
Offset Left 28 (remember the 3 back's assignment on a non-lead call)
Offset Right fake 38, 44 dive

Beast formation. When you want to take advantage of the blocking abilities of your fullbacks the Beast formation is very effective. It can be called to the left or right. The Beast formation only affects the fullbacks (backs 2 and 4). On a "Beast Left" call the 4 back lines up to the left of the LE and off of the line of scrimmage.

This formation lends itself to the power sweep. Imagine a call of "Beast Left 37 sweep." This formation has both fullbacks leading the charge for your best runner. Basically this call is designed to match your best athletes against the defense.

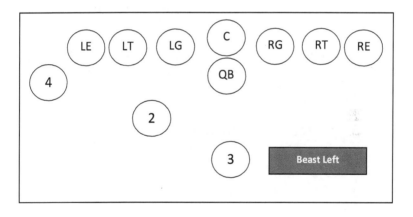

Unlike the Offset formation the Beast formation can be called to both sides. Take a look at the formation when a "Beast Left and Beast right" is called. You can rename the 'both' call if you plan on using it more. Have fun with naming as we are coaching kids (Big Beast, Doubled Fanged Beast, Wolverine...). Some of the more experienced youth coaches will recognize this formation as a Double Wing.

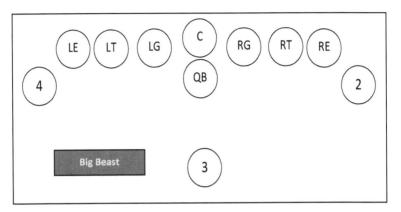

Instruct your fullbacks that if this formation is called their blocking assignments change. Back 4 will lead any sweep to the left and back 2 will lead any sweep to the right. If an inside run is called they are to prevent any outside-in pursuit.

The 'Big Beast' formation can also be a great way to introduce your team to 'Motion' calls. You can call the 4 back to go in motion prior to receiving a handoff or to add another blocker to a sweep.

A typical QB cadence is in three commands. Ours usually is "Down, Set, Hut." During the QB cadence have the QB signal the motion player after 'Down, Set.' A simple signal like the stomping of one foot will suffice. Teach the QB to be patient with the motion player and make sure they are in position before hiking the ball.

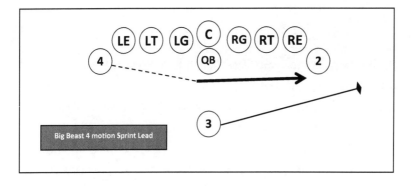

From a 'Big Beast' formation you can call many of the same plays.

48 Lead
32 Dive
Fake 38, 17

The Beast formation can also be set up from a shift. Have your team line up in the standard Diamond formation. The full backs in their normal position behind the 3 and 4 gaps. When the QB begins his cadence have the Fullback(s) sprint to his/their Beast position. A typical QB cadence is in three commands. Ours usually is "Down, Set, Hut." On 'Down' the Fullbacks would sprint to their new position. The QB would make sure they were in place before he commanded 'Set.' Make sure the QB knows that the shifting players have to be set for a full second before the ball is snapped.

A shift can confuse a defense so make sure your shifting players understand the urgency of the maneuver. In practice make sure they sprint, and do not jog, to their new positions.

Split formation. So the defense is keying back 3 as they have figured out he is the best athlete at running back. Knowing that back 3 is the best athlete the defense instructs their best athlete to mirror him. Now it is time to call a split formation. The Split formation is designed for the 3 back alone and can be called to the left or right. When a Split formation is called the 3 back becomes a wide out.

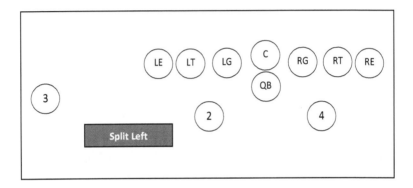

A number plays can be called from the split formation depending on the defense. If the defense is mirroring back 3 with their best athlete (usually a MLB or Safety type) we can grind the defense on a series of 23 and 44 dives. Or sweep away from him with a "Split Left 28 Sweep."

Isolating the defenses best athlete is only one consideration when calling a Split formation. If the defense has a good DE we can sweep towards back 3. Instruct back 3 that any sweep towards him he should ignore the man over him and block down towards the defensive line in an attempt to block pursuing defenders. The lead full back should follow his assignment and crossover the 3 back and kick out the defender that lined up over the 3 back.

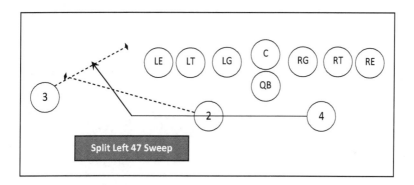

When calling a Split formation instruct your QB and back 3 to be aware of who lines up over the split back. Since the majority of our formations are tight and rarely do we have the back or other players split out you may catch the defense confused. If the 3 back gets out to his split position and no defender follows him, or lines up over him, instruct him not to set up in the standard receiver stance. Instead have him turn and face the QB. If the QB sees no one is out with the 3 back and he has turned to face him then the QB is to ignore the play called and pass it to back 3.

The Split formation can also be used as a shift from the standard formation. One concern is the amount of time it takes the 3 back to get from directly behind the QB to a split position.

Spread Formation. The Spread Formation signals the Ends to step away from the line by 2 steps, step back from the line, and assume a 2 point receiver stance. The Fullbacks spread out from the Ends about 5 steps and assume a 2 point receiver stance on the line of scrimmage.

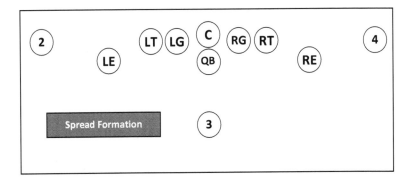

From the Spread formation we have a number of new options. If we are running sweep right (38 Pitch) or sweep left (37 Pitch) we can have our Fullback block down towards the defensive line, usually to wall in the defensive end, while the End leads the charge around the Fullback.

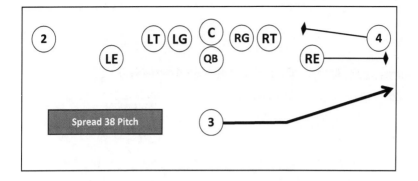

If you want to add a pre-snap motion the Spread formation is a great way to do just that. Try a 'Spread X motion 38 pitch.'

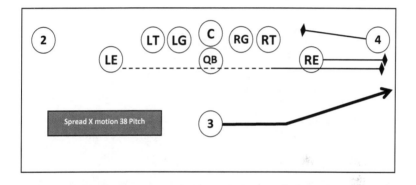

The Spread formation is an excellent call to use a shift. Imagine the defense scrambling to the call 'Shift Spread X Motion 38 Pitch.'

Combining the formations. As your players get comfortable with the different formation calls we can start combining formation calls. A great aspect of the system design is that most formation calls are meant only for certain players. This allows the players to quickly grasp multiple formation calls. Only the 3 back responds to the 'Split' call. Only the tackles respond to the 'Offset' calls. Only the full backs respond to the 'Beast' call.

We can take the overload of one side even further with "Offset Left, Beast Left, 37 Sweep."

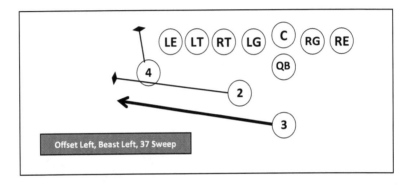

The Triple Threat play is designed to be run several times in a game and starts from the base Diamond formation. It has six separate calls designed to look alike and confuse the defense. When run correctly it has three separate run options (two fakes and the actual runner) each play. It can be called to either side on the diamond formation and consists of a fullback dive, a tailback counter (with a full back lead block), and a quarterback keeper. I would label the call either 'Rhino,' right, or 'Leopard,' left. The direction, right or left, signals which way the quarterback will turn to initiate the play.

There are six calls for the Triple Threat.

Rhino Dive
Rhino Counter
Rhino Keeper
Leopard Dive
Leopard Counter
Leopard Keeper

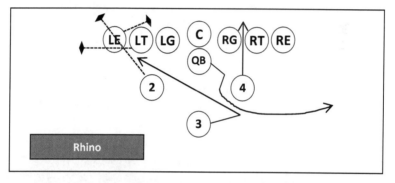

A) If Rhino (right) is called the quarterback opens to his right and takes a step away from the line angling towards the fullback. The fullback is the first threat. The fullback (4 back) opens his arms for the ball and dives forward through the 4 gap. If the call was 'Rhino Dive' he would be the actual runner. If not he steams ahead as if he was (fake). Whether this is the fake or not, the quarterback makes this handoff with both hands on the ball until the last possible second. Regardless if the fullback was the actual runner the rest of the backfield will continue with the play as if the fullback was the fake. The 3 back initiates a counter run. He steps to his right so that the 4 gap, fullback, and tailback are all in line.

B) Next, the quarterback pulls his arms back and pivots to his right just enough to shield the ball from the defense's view. The quarterback, with the ball shielded, extends his right arm and tucks his left. If the call is 'Rhino counter' he has the ball in his right hand and if the call was 'Rhino keeper' he would have the ball tucked in his left. The 3 back, who is now behind the 4 back, cuts back towards the 5 gap.

C) If the call was 'Rhino counter' the 3 back runs through the extended right arm of the quarterback, takes the ball, and follows the 2 back through the 5 gap. The cross block is good fit for the counter. On the triple threat calls have the End and Tackle cross block for the counter play. On Rhino calls the left end and tackle cross block.

D) If the call was 'Rhino keeper' the quarterback would have the ball tucked in his left hand. The 3 back runs through his extended right hand and continues towards the 5 gap. Once back 3 passes by the quarterback the QB sprints out to the right side or 8 gap.

When run correctly the triple threat causes a defense to hesitate or key on the wrong back. This confusion favors the offense that is prepared and running with confidence.

When introducing this series of plays I have the backs run a drill without the ball. The challenge I place on them is to convince me (coaches) that they are running their assignments as if they have the ball.

When running the drill critique how fast they run without a ball and if any of their movements are over exaggerated. Watch for the following trends that players seem to universally do when faking.

- The runner's arms are open far wider when they fake.
- They exaggerate the snapping down on a handoff.
- They crouch much lower when faking to run then when they are actually carrying the ball.
- Players tend to 'jog' rather than run when they are faking.

Run the initial drills without the ball and correct these common mistakes. Introduce the ball to the drill when everyone is running their assignments 'as if' they have the ball. Full speed and not over exaggerated is what you need from the backfield.

The Triple Threat is a system all on to its self. You could literally run one of the six calls every play and if your team is running it with confidence and in a disciplined manner it becomes difficult to stop.

If your team has the basics down for the Triple Threat you can add another threat. Have the Tight End on the called side (Rhino for the Right End) initiate a down block. Then turn back and run a side line route. This gives the QB a final option if a Keeper is called. If the QB finds the LBs and/or DBs crashing down on him he can pass it to the TE who is running a pass route about five yards beyond the line of scrimmage.

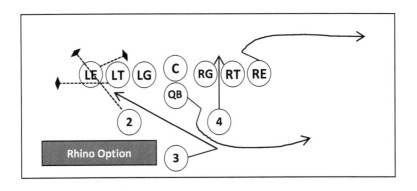

Your Turn.

On the surface this system seems simple. However, it is only a tool of the play caller. As a coach you will have to experiment with what *your* team does best. As this system prepares youth football players to get quickly integrated into the offense it is the coach that has to master the offense. If you are a first year coach or a seasoned veteran this system will assist you in having a strong offense, but you have to be the one who calls the plays.

Familiarize yourself with the offense before introducing The Diamond Formation Power Running System to your team. Ask yourself what type of team do you have? How good are your skill players? How tough is your line? I would suggest sitting down and drawing out the different possibilities this system gives you.

I have supplied the skeleton of the offense for you. It is time for you to add the muscle.

As a coach you are going to ask your players to work hard and focus. Now is the time to give them back that same effort.

Here is your homework assignment:

1. Get a blank paper and pencil and draw up the following plays;
    a. 34
    b. Fake 37, 18 Keeper
    c. 28

      d. 47 Lead
      e. Leopard Keeper
      f. Split Left, Fake 47, X sprint
      g. Split Right, Offset Left, Beast right, 43
      h. Beast Left 48 Lead
2. Draw up the first 10 plays, in sequence, you will run in a practice or a game.
      a. Have you utilized all your weapons?
      b. Is the sequence predictable?

How did you do? The idea is to train yourself to call plays quickly. We are asking our players to play fast so we have to be prepared to call plays quickly. Try mental exercises like the one above to get yourself to 'see' the plays without having to consult a tangible playbook during a game. Doing so will aid your team on getting in and out of the huddle quickly. Do everything you can to keep the defense guessing.

Now get out there and coach.

If you have any questions your comments you can email me at coach@dennisserra.com. I am busy so I may not get back to you immediately, but I will try to as soon as I can.

Made in the USA
San Bernardino, CA
08 January 2019